DOLPHINS SET I

SPINNER DOLPHINS

Megan M. Gunderson
ABDO Publishing Company

visit us at
www.abdopublishing.com

Published by ABDO Publishing Company, 8000 West 78th Street, Edina, Minnesota 55439. Copyright © 2011 by Abdo Consulting Group, Inc. International copyrights reserved in all countries. No part of this book may be reproduced in any form without written permission from the publisher. The Checkerboard Library™ is a trademark and logo of ABDO Publishing Company.

Printed in the United States of America, North Mankato, Minnesota.
042010
092010

 PRINTED ON RECYCLED PAPER

Cover Photo: Photolibrary
Interior Photos: Alamy pp. 8, 15, 21; © James D. Watt / SeaPics.com p. 19;
    © Michael S. Nolan / SeaPics.com p. 13; National Geographic Stock p. 5;
    Peter Arnold p. 17; Uko Gorter pp. 7, 9

Editor: BreAnn Rumsch
Art Direction & Cover Design: Neil Klinepier

Library of Congress Cataloging-in-Publication Data

Gunderson, Megan M., 1981-
  Spinner dolphins / Megan M. Gunderson.
      p. cm. -- (Dolphins)
  Includes index.
  ISBN 978-1-61613-414-3
  1. Stenella longirostris--Juvenile literature. I. Title.
  QL737.C432G8596 2010
  599.53'4--dc22
                              2010001590

CONTENTS

SPINNER DOLPHINS

Spinner dolphins are named for the exciting way they behave above water. These **cetaceans** twirl like acrobats as they fly through the air!

Like all cetaceans, spinner dolphins are mammals. That means they are **warm-blooded** and nurse their young. Spinner dolphins swim to the ocean's surface to breathe. They take in air through a blowhole at the top of the head.

Scientists currently recognize four spinner dolphin **subspecies**. These are the Gray's spinner, the eastern spinner, the Central American spinner, and the dwarf spinner. The whitebelly spinner dolphin is a cross between the Gray's spinner and the eastern spinner. All spinner dolphins belong to the family **Delphinidae**.

Spinner dolphins are abundant in Earth's warm ocean waters.

SIZE, SHAPE, AND COLOR

A spinner dolphin's size depends on its **subspecies**. Average adults weigh 165 pounds (75 kg). They grow six to eight feet (1.8 to 2.4 m) long. Females are slightly smaller than males.

The spinner dolphin has a slim, **streamlined** body. It has a tall dorsal fin, small flukes, and pointed flippers. Its long, narrow beak is set off from the forehead by a crease.

Other features set apart each subspecies. The eastern spinner's dorsal fin slopes forward with age. On the Gray's spinner, it may curve slightly backward. Male eastern and Central American spinners have a distinctive hump. It is in front of the flukes on the belly side.

BEAK

MELON

GRAY'S SPINNER DOLPHIN

DORSAL FIN

FLIPPERS

Central American and eastern spinners are almost solid gray. Other spinners have three stripes of color. The back is dark gray, and the sides are pale gray. The belly is light gray or white. The beak is gray on top and white on the bottom. It has a dark tip.

FLUKES

Where They Live

Spinner dolphins live in **tropical** and **subtropical** waters. They are found in the Atlantic, Pacific, and Indian oceans. The four **subspecies** live in different areas. However, some of their ranges **overlap**.

Central American spinners are found from southern Mexico to Costa Rica.

Gray's spinner dolphins live in the Atlantic and Indian oceans. They also call the western and central Pacific Ocean home. They live offshore around islands.

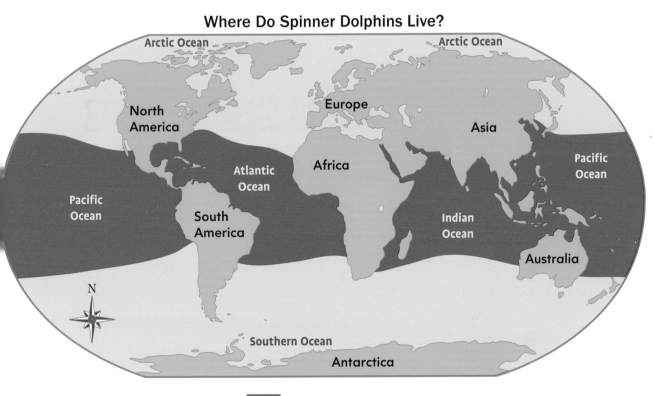

Where Do Spinner Dolphins Live?

spinner dolphins

Eastern spinners live offshore in the eastern Pacific Ocean. Central American spinners also live in the eastern Pacific. However, they prefer the coastal waters of the **continental shelf**. Dwarf spinners live in coastal waters, too. They are found from Southeast Asia to Australia.

SENSES

Keen senses help spinner dolphins survive in their huge ocean home. Spinner dolphins have great eyesight. In fact, they can see well in or out of water.

Spinner dolphins also have an excellent sense of touch. And, they can taste their food. However, scientists do not believe dolphins have a sense of smell.

A great sense of hearing is important for communication. Spinner dolphins make whistling noises. They also listen for them. Each dolphin's whistle is individual. This helps them identify each other.

Hearing also helps dolphins with echolocation. Spinner dolphins use this system to navigate underwater.

A dolphin sends out a series of clicks through its **melon**. These hit any object in the dolphin's path and bounce back. The dolphin listens for these returning echoes. They tell it the object's size, shape, speed, distance, and direction.

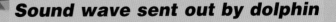

Sound wave sent out by dolphin

Echo wave received by dolphin

DEFENSE

Spinner dolphins face danger from both natural predators and humans. Tiger sharks, cookie-cutter sharks, and killer whales attack spinner dolphins. Short-finned pilot whales, false killer whales, and pygmy killer whales also pose a threat.

Speed is one defense spinner dolphins have against predators. They can swim more than 17 miles per hour (28 km/h). Staying together as a group also provides protection.

Echolocation warns dolphins of nearby threats. To communicate danger to others, spinner dolphins use their whistles.

Unfortunately, spinner dolphins often cannot escape dangers posed by humans. Tuna nets may trap and drown dolphins. Changes in fishing practices have lowered the number of spinner dolphins killed in nets. Yet, many are still accidentally caught.

Cookie-cutter sharks take round bites out of their prey.

FOOD

Most spinner dolphins feed on squid, shrimps, and small fish. Dwarf spinners prefer to eat bottom-dwelling and coral reef animals.

Spinner dolphins often hunt their prey at night. To organize the hunt, spinners communicate underwater using their whistle sounds.

To find prey, spinner dolphins use echolocation. Then, they work as a group to herd it. To catch their prey, spinners will dive down 650 to 1,000 feet (200 to 300 m).

Spinner dolphins use their small, cone-shaped teeth to grab their food. There are up to 128 teeth in the upper jaw. The lower jaw holds up to 124 teeth. All those teeth are made for gripping prey, not chewing. Dolphins swallow their food whole!

Spinner dolphins work together to find and capture prey.

BABIES

Mating occurs year-round for spinner dolphins. After mating, a female spinner dolphin is **pregnant** for 10 to 11 months. She almost always gives birth to a single baby dolphin. It is called a calf.

At birth, a spinner calf is about 28 to 34 inches (70 to 85 cm) long. It weighs around 22 pounds (10 kg). Like other mammals, the mother dolphin makes milk for her calf. The calf will nurse for one to two years.

Spinner dolphins form nursery groups to help raise a calf. Each group includes adult females and large males. They help keep the calf safe. The calf also learns from them as it grows into an adult. A spinner dolphin may live for 23 years.

On average, a mother spinner dolphin will wait three years before having another calf.

BEHAVIORS

Spinner dolphins live in groups. In the open ocean, groups contain thousands of members! Near shore, they are smaller. At night, these smaller groups may join together. Then, the large group heads out to hunt.

Wherever spinner dolphins gather, spinning is their best-known feature. Scientists are still studying why they do it. Some believe it has to do with communication.

Spinner dolphins leap up to ten feet (3 m) into the air. They can spin as many as seven times per jump. And, they will make up to 14 jumps in a row.

Near shore, spinner dolphins are also active around ships. They are curious animals that like to **bow ride**. Spinner dolphins also do somersaults in midair. These playful, speedy dolphins are a treat to see!

SPINNER DOLPHIN FACTS

Scientific Name: *Stenella longirostris*

Common Names: Spinner dolphin, Gray's spinner dolphin, Hawaiian spinner dolphin, eastern spinner dolphin, dwarf spinner dolphin, Central American spinner dolphin, whitebelly spinner dolphin

Average Size: Adult spinner dolphins grow six to eight feet (1.8 to 2.4 m) long. They weigh around 165 pounds (75 kg). Males are slightly larger than females.

Where They're Found: In tropical and subtropical waters of the Atlantic, Pacific, and Indian oceans

GLOSSARY

bow ride - to swim at the front of a boat or a whale. A dolphin uses the waves created there to assist movement and speed.

cetacean (sih-TAY-shuhn) - a member of the order Cetacea. Mammals such as dolphins, whales, and porpoises are cetaceans.

continental shelf - a shallow, underwater plain forming a continent's border. It ends with a steep slope to the deep ocean floor.

Delphinidae (dehl-FIHN-uh-dee) - the scientific name for the oceanic dolphin family. It includes dolphins that live mostly in salt water.

melon - a rounded structure found in the forehead of some cetaceans.

overlap - to occupy the same area in part.

pregnant - having one or more babies growing within the body.

streamlined - designed to offer the least possible resistance to air or water.

subspecies - a group of related organisms ranking below a species. Members of a subspecies often share a common geographic range.

subtropical - relating to an area where average temperatures range between 55 and 68 degrees Fahrenheit (13 and 20°C).

tropical - relating to an area with an average temperature above 77 degrees Fahrenheit (25°C) where no freezing occurs.

warm-blooded - having a body temperature that is not much affected by surrounding air or water.

WEB SITES

To learn more about spinner dolphins, visit ABDO Publishing Company on the World Wide Web at **www.abdopublishing.com**. Web sites about spinner dolphins are featured on our Book Links page. These links are routinely monitored and updated to provide the most current information available.

INDEX